The Kings and Queens of England

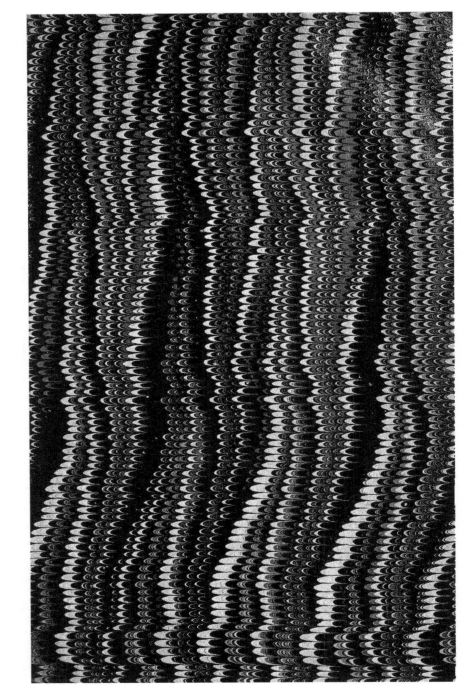

THE

KINGS AND QUEENS OF ENGLAND

WITH

OTHER POEMS:

BY

1871

MARY ANN H. T BIGELOW.

BOSTON:
PUBLISHED FOR THE AUTHOR,
BY S K WHIPPLE AND COMPANY
MDCCCLIII

PRESS OF GEO. C. LAND

CORNHILL

TO THE

COMPANION OF HER YOUTH, MIDDLE AGE, AND DECLINING YEARS,

THE FOLLOWING POEMS ARE INSCRIBED

BY HIS

AFFECTIONATE WIFE,

MARY ANN H T BIGELOW

PREFACE.

I must claim the indulgence of my friends for the many defects they will find in my poems, which they will please wink at, remembering that I was sixty years old when I commenced rhyming ; and this by way of experiment, while on a visit to my daughter, in Brooklyn

My first essay, was The Monarchs of England. I took it up for my amusement, wishing to ascertain how much of that history I could recollect without help from any other source than memory

The rhyme is in many places far from smooth, and there are many redundances that might with advantage be lopped off , and were it to come under the critic's eye to be reviewed, I should feel it quite necessary to improve it, (the poetry, I mean.) But as it would require quite too much exertion for my eyes in their present state, and as the history, dates, &c., I believe, are correct, I send it to the press " with all its imperfections on its head."

CONTENTS.

POEMS.

THE KINGS AND QUEENS OF ENGLAND,

FROM THE BATTLE OF HASTINGS OR THE NORMAN CONQUEST,
TO THE PRESENT REIGN, INCLUSIVE

FIRST, William the Norman lays claim to the crown
And retains it till death; then follows his son
The red headed William, whose life is cut short
By a shot from his friend, when hunting for sport.
Then Henry his brother takes quiet possession,
As Henry the first, of the great English nation.
Next Stephen, a kinsman gets the crown by his might,
But no one pretends to say he had a right.
Then comes Hal the second, who cuts a great figure
With Becket, fair Rosamond and Queen Eliner.

B

The Lion-hearted *Richard*, first of that name,
Succeeded his father in power and in fame;
He joined the Crusade to a far distant land
But his life was cut short by a murderous hand.
Next comes the *cruel* and *cowardly* John,
From whose hand, reluctant, Magna Charta was won.
Then his son Henry third, deny it who can?
Though unfit for a King, was yet a good man,
And his reign though a long one of fifty-six years
Was full of perplexities, sorrows, and fears.
His son Edward first next governs the nation,
Much respected and feared, in holding that station.
The Principality of Wales was annexed in his reign,
And his son Edward second, first Prince of that name.
But what shall I say of King Edward the third,
The most remarkable reign, that yet had occurred;
Fire arms in the war, were *first* used in his reign,
And the battle of *Cressy* of great note and fame,
To their introduction has the right to lay claim.
The knights of the Garter, first made in his reign
In honor it seems of a fair English dame,
The Duchess of Salisbury to whom it is said,
From Edward *peculiar* attentions were paid.

Of Richard the second we have little to say,
And take up the fourth Henry, the next on our way,
Who reigned fourteen years, when death cut him down
And left his good Kingdom to Henry his son;
But ere nine years had past, the fifth Henry was borne
To the region of darkness from whence none return.
The next reign is full of commotion and strife,
And Henry the sixth is seen flying for life;
For though King of England, we cannot but see
He's but the shadow of a king — that *should* be;
And during the thirty-nine years that he reigned
His crown and his sceptre were feebly retained.
It was in this reign on her mission intent,
That Joan of Arc to the battle field went:
The French troops were elated, the English dismayed
At the wonderful victories achieved by her aid;
At length fortune turns, and 'tis needless to tell
Of the fate of this maiden — it is all known too well
Of Edward the fourth it seems proper to say
That he fancied Dame Shore, when wed to Bess Gray
But the fate of Jane Shore, should be warning to all
Who from love, or ambition, are tempted to fall.

When Edward the fourth departed this earth,
He left two little sons, both Royal by birth;
But ere three years had pass'd, both met with their
        doom,
By a most cruel uncle, cut down in their bloom
Of youth, love, and beauty, and laid in the tomb.
King Edward the fifth was the eldest one's name,
Though never permitted by his uncle to reign.
Next comes cruel Richard, the third of that name,
Whose vices surpassing put others to shame.
When unhorsed in battle, he's so anxious to live,
That he cries " for a horse, my kingdom I'll give."
But in the same battle he had his last fall —
Lamented by none, but detested by all.
In the next reign the wars of the roses, all ended,
And the red rose and white, forever were blended;
For when Henry the seventh took Bessy his bride,
The knot of the roses forever was tied;
And when the sceptre descended from father to son,
The red and the white leaves all mingled in one.
King Henry the eighth had quite a long reign
Mixed up with his Anne's, his Katy's and Jane.

But from this King we turn with disgust and with
      shame,
And greet with delight, the sixth Edward by name.
But only six years did this King fill the throne,
When called to resign it and lay his crown down.
A worthier we think, has never set
On the throne of Great Britain — at least not as yet.
With pleasure we love to contemplate him now,
With a bright crown of Glory, encircling his brow,
In the region of *light, love, peace,* and of joy,
Where pleasures eternal can have no alloy.
Sin, sickness, and death, never find entrance there,
For the air is all balm, and the skies ever fair;
The clouds of his young life have all passed away
And he enjoys the full light of an endless day —
For all who find footing on that peaceful shore,
Shall hunger, and thirst, and sorrow no more.
But once more we return to this " dim speck of earth,"
And revisit the clime that gave Edward his birth.
Bloody Mary his sister, next mounted the throne,
But when five years had pass'd, was obliged to lay
      down,
Notwithstanding reluctance, her Sceptre and Crown.

For death to whom she had sent many a one,
Now called for his victim, and made her his own.
Not by *fire* and by *faggot* was *she* hurried away,
But by painful sickness and loathsome decay.
Now commences the reign of the "Good Queen Bess,"
But *why* she's called *good* I never could guess:
Yet justice constrains me to allow in the main,
That her's was a glorious and most prosperous reign.
She had the good sense to know whom to admit
To her private councils, as men the most fit;
And by their advice, good sense and discretion,
She managed with *fitness* to govern the nation.
As a Queen she seems great, though *weak* as a woman,
And when praised as a *Goddess*, was no more than
  human;
At the age of threescore, she loved to be compared
As a beauty to Venus, though crook'd and red haired.
Of lovers she had full many a one,
Who sought, through her hand, a pass to the throne,
But chose to remain single; for full well she knew,
That in giving her hand, she gave away her power too.
In this reign we find ineffacible blots,
In the treatment of Essex, and Mary of Scots;

The death of the former, the Queen sorely repents,
And for her lost Essex she deeply laments.
The remorse of a Countess, in keeping his ring,
I leave to some rhymer, more able to sing.
Next James sixth of Scotland, *first* of England became
In peace and security permitted to reign.
In the person of James, two crowns were united,
And England and Scotland remain undivided.
With this king the reign of the Stuarts began,
And continued to the end of the reign of Queen Ann.
In the reign of Charles first, commences a strife
Between King and Parliament, that ends but with life;
This poor King was beheaded, his son had to flee,
And in his place Oliver Cromwell we see.
Now in Cromwell the ruler of England we find;
Right or wrong, I never could make up my mind;
Still all must allow (for deny it who can?)
That this same Oliver was a very great man.
In eleven years the days of the Commonwealth ended,
And gay Charles the second, the throne then ascended.
This second king Charles king of hearts might be
          call'd,
For many a fair one he seems t' have enthrall'd.

James second, brother of Charles second succeeded,
But after a reign of four years, he seceded;
When quitting his throne, and his country he flies
Over the channel to France, where he dies.
Next the Prince of Orange, (from Holland he came,)
For the crown of old England, asserted his claim
Through right of his wife, Princess Mary by name.
And William the third with Mary his wife
Are crowned King and Queen of England for life.
This princess was lovely in person and mind,
As a wife most devoted, a *friend ever* kind.
Queen Ann's is the next reign that in order appears
And it covers the space of thirteen full years.
Her death brought the reign of the Stuarts to a close,
But firm on their ruins, the House of Hanover rose.
With this house the reign of the Georges begins —
And four in succession we count up as Kings.
George the third, grandson of the second, so called,
Was for virtues and goodness of heart much extolled.
His reign the longest of any appears,
Bearing title of king for sixty-two years.
But when aged four score, this good king we find
Bereft of his senses and hearing, and blind.

In this reign America declared herself free,
And independent of rulers over the sea.
At length death relieved him, and he was cut down,
To make way for his eldest and libertine son.
But though of talent acknowledged the son possessed
    more,
The *sire's heart was good,* the *son's corrupt at the core ;*
Though admired for his beauty, and manners, and wit,
As a husband and father he never was fit.
But before we pass on to the next reign in course,
We have a most sorrowful tale to rehearse,
Of the young princess Charlotte, next heir to the crown,
In the spring time of life, scarce with warning cut
    down.
If ever the nation were mourners sincere,
.'T was when they united around the sad bier
Of this youthful princess so deservedly dear ;
And stout-hearted men unaccustomed to mourn,
Let bitter tears fall, as they gazed on her urn.
But who can describe the anguish of one,
The heart-stricken husband apart and alone.
As the sun of his happiness rose to its height,
Death enters his dwelling, and lo ! it is night ;

The light of his house forever has fled,

For his loved one, his dearest, lies low with the dead.

In the *same* day all his fair prospects were crossed,

When a *wife*, and a *son*, and a *kingdom* he lost.

Next William the fourth, is proclaimed Britain's king,

For between him and his brother two deaths intervene.

No *legitimate* child did he leave in possession

Of the Crown of old England, in right of succession ;

So the diadem passed to the youthful brow

Of his niece Queen Victoria, who honors it now ;

And for her we wish, as our rhyming we close,

A *long, peaceful reign* — an old age of repose.

Written while on a visit at Brooklyn, N Y , 1851.

TO MY DAUGHTER ELIZABETH.

Two flowers upon one parent stem
Together bloomed for many days,
At length a storm arose, and *one*
Was blighted, and cut down at noon.

The other hath transplanted been,
And flowers *fair* as *herself* hath borne;
She too has felt the withering storm,
Her strength's decayed, wasted her form.

May he who hears the mourner's prayer,
Renew her strength for years to come;
Long may He our Lilly spare,
Long delay to call her home.

But when the summons shall arrive
To bear this lovely flower away,
Again may she transplanted be
To blossom in eternity.

There may these sisters meet again,
Both freed from sorrow, sin, and pain;
There with united voices raise,
In sweet accord their hymns of praise;
Eternally his name t' adore,
Who died, yet *lives forevermore.*

Weston, Jan 3, 1852

ACROSTIC.

For thee, my son, a mother's earnest prayer
Rises to Heaven each day from heart sincere,
Anxiously seeking what concerns thee most;
Not merely earthly good for thee she prays,
Knowledge, or wealth, or fame, or length of days,
What shall these profit, if the soul be lost.

In this life we find alternate day and night,
Not always darkness, *sure not always* light;
'T is well it should be so, we 're travellers here,
Home, *that* "sweet home," the Christian's place of rest,
Rises by faith to view when most distressed:
Oh! this life past — mayst thou find entrance there.

Perplexed, distressed, sick, or by friends betrayed,
Beset with snares, deprived of human aid,
In all thy sorrows whatsoe'er they be,
Go to the Saviour, tell him all thy need,
Entreat his pity, he 's a friend indeed ;
Lay hold by faith on *Him*, and he will succor thee.
Oh, do not live for this dull world alone,
When with the *Angels* thou mayst find a home.

Jan. 1853

THE EVENING OF LIFE.

As the shadows of evening around me are falling,
With its dark sombre curtain outspread,
And night 's just at hand, chilly night so appalling,
And day's brilliant sunshine hath fled,

It is e'en so with me, for the eve of my day
Has arrived, yet I scarcely know how;
Bright morn hath departed, and noon passed away,
And 't is evening, *pale* eve with me now.

Oh! where are the friends who in life's early morn,
With me did their journey commence;
Some are estranged, while some few still remain,
And others departed long since.

And when I too, like them, shall be summoned away,
And the shadows of death on me fall,
Be thou the Great Shepherd of Israel but near,
My Saviour, my God, and my all.

And though the "dark valley" we all must pass
    through,
Yet surely no evil can harm
The *sheep*, when the Shepherd is walking there too,
And supports them by his mighty arm.

Oh! my Redeemer, wilt thou be with me then,
And food for my journey provide,
Divide the dark waters of Jordan again,
And safe in thy bosom me hide.

Though wild beasts of the desert may roar long and
    loud,
And the billows of ocean rise high,
With thy rod and thy staff for my strength and support,
I shall pass them in safety all by.

And having crossed Jordan, on Canaan's bright shore
With what joy shall I take a survey,
And reflect that the dangers of life are all o'er,
And with unclouded vision enjoy evermore
The bright sun of an endless day.

Weston, Feb 4, 1852

D

AN ACROSTIC.

Merry, merry little child,
Active, playful, sometimes wild;
Rosy cheeks, and ringlets rare,
Glossy black, with eyes compare.
All, *all* these belong to thee,
Right pleasant little Margerie.
Every good, dear child, be given
Thee on earth, and rest in heaven.
But who thy future lot can see?
All, *every* page is hid from me;
Xtended through eternity,
Thy life so late begun will be.
Earnest seek to know the truth,
Remember God in early youth;
When in his sacred courts thou art,
Engage in worship thy *whole heart;*

Listen to what the preacher says,
Listen to prayers, and list to praise,
In nothing see thou dost offend,
Nor fail the Sabbath *well* to spend.
Give to thy parents honor due,
Thy sisters love, and brothers too;
Oh ! good and happy mayst thou be,
Now and ever, Margerie.

AN ACROSTIC.

Cannot happiness perfect be found on this earth?
How absurd to expect it — sin comes with our birth.
As soon from spring bitter, sweet water procure,
Rich clusters of grapes from the thorn;
Look for figs upon thistles, when seeking for food,
Or bread from the cold flinty stone.
The wealth of the Indies, *true* peace can't bestow,
The Crown Royal oft presses an aching brow,
E'en in laughter there's madness — mirth coupled with
     woe.

As true peace in this world, then, can never be found,
Until deep in the heart Christian graces abound,
Give diligent heed to the keeping thy heart;
Unwearied in effort, repel every dart
So dextrously pointed by Satan's black art.

True peace is from Heaven — a child of the skies,
And feeble exertions secure not the prize.

Never falter in duty, but trust in that power
Engaged to support you in each trying hour ;
When sinking like Peter amidst the dark wave,
Ever look unto Jesus, almighty to save.
Look *to* him, live *like* him, be strong in his might,
Lay thy *burden* on him, and thy *cross* he 'll make light.

WRITTEN UPON RECEIVING A NEW YEAR'S GIFT.

I have a little Grandchild dear,
Who sends to me on each new year
    A valuable present:
Not costly gift from store-house bought,
But one that her own hands have wrought,
    Therefore to me more pleasant.

Accept, dear child, the wish sincere,
For you much happiness this year,
    And length of days be given ;
Here may you act well your part,
Serving the Lord with all your heart,
    And find your rest in heaven.

Jan 1852

LINES

TO THE MEMORY OF PATRICK KELLEY, WHO BY HIS MANY GOOD QUALI-
TIES DURING SOME YEARS' RESIDENCE IN MY FAMILY, GREATLY
ENDEARED HIMSELF TO ME AND MINE

From Erin's fair Isle to this country he came,
And found brothers and sisters to welcome him here;
Though then but a youth, yet robust seemed his frame,
And life promised fair for many a long year.

A place was soon found where around the same board,
He with two of his sisters did constantly meet;
And when his day's work had all been performed,
At the *same* fireside he found a third seat.

His faithfulness such, so true-hearted was he,
That love in return could not be denied;
As one of the family — he soon ceased to be
The stranger, who lately for work had applied.

Youth passed into manhood, and with it there came
New duties to fill, new plans to pursue;
But a fatal disease now seizes his frame,
And with health is his strength fast leaving him too.

From his home in the country to the city he went,
Where kind brothers procured him good medical aid;
But all was in vain — Death commissioned was sent,
And soon his remains in the cold grave were laid.

The broad waves of Atlantic lie rolling between
His brothers and sisters and parents on earth;
And never by parents may those children be seen,
Or the latter revisit the land of their birth.

But sooner or later they all must be borne
To that region of darkness from whence none return;
Oh! then may they meet on Canaan's bright shore,
An *unbroken household* to part nevermore.

Weston, Jan 1852

MY S. S. CLASS.

I now will endeavor, while fresh in my mind,
My Sabbath School Class to portray;
The theme 's furnished for me, I 've only to find
Colors to blend, their forms to display.

And first on the canvass we 'll Adeline place,
With her full and expressive dark eye;
Decision of purpose is stamped on that face,
And good scholarship too we descry.

Next in order comes Alice, with bright sunny smile,
That does one's heart good to behold;
May the sorrows of life ne'er that young spirit blight,
Nor that heart be less cheerful when old.

F.

But who 's this that we see, with that mild pensive air,
And a look so expressively kind ?
It is Ann, gentle Ann, before whom we pass by,
We will add — 't would be useless in any to try
Disposition more lovely to find.

The next is a bright noble face we espy,
'T is a boy of ten years we shall find ;
There 's a spice of the rogue in that merry young eye,
With good sense and good nature combined.

It 's young master Alpheus — we never have found
One more punctual at school hour than he ;
He 's now but a lad, yet who knows when a *man,*
But a *Judge in our land* he may be.

Next comes little Moggy, our dear little Moggy,
But before she is brought out to view,
We 'll new colors select, add fresh tints to the whole,
And spread all on our pallet anew.

And now she appears in her own proper size,
Her cheeks colored by nature's warm glow ;

With her full lustrous and speaking black eyes,
And rich ringlets that grace her young brow.

Walter 's the last on the painting we see,
Little Walter, the youngest of all ;
Look ! he 's repeating his lesson just now,
Mark the expression on that infant brow,
He 's a *wonder*, for scholar so small.

But there 's one in this grouping we look for in vain,
Whose image we often recall ;
How mournfully sweet is the sound of thy name,
Dear Elbridge, the loved one of all.

Thou wert called in the freshness of morning away,
By him who all things doeth well ;
The rest for brief periods are suffered to stay,
How long, we may none of us tell.

May the Holy Book studied in this Sabbath School,
Be more precious than silver or gold ;
Be its doctrines received, and its precepts obeyed,
And *rich treasures* it still will unfold.

And when one by one we shall all pass away,
To me, oh! my Father, be given
The joy that no heart upon earth can conceive,
To meet all in the kingdom of Heaven.

Weston, Feb 17, 1852.

FOR MY GRANDSONS, EDDY AND ALLY.

I here engage
Upon this page
    A picture to portray,
Of two of an age
Yet neither a sage,
    But right honest hearts have they.
Each loves to play
And have his own way,
Yet I 'm happy to say
    They quarrel, if ever, but seldom.
Though competent quite
To maintain their own right,
And even to fight,
    Yet peace to their bosom is welcome.
Both go to school,
And learn by rule

That in neither a dunce we may find ,
Both read and spell
And like it well ;
    Thus with pleasure is profit combined.
One's eyes are black,
The other's blue ;
    They both have honest hearts and true,
    And love each other dearly .
One's father, is brother
To the other one's mother,
    So cousins german are they most clearly .
Each has a father,
And each has a mother,
    And both do dearly love him ;
But neither a sister,
And neither a brother,
    To *play* with, or to *plague* him.
And here I propose,
Ere I come to a close,
    A little advice to give ;
To which if they heed,
They 'll be better indeed,
    And happier as long as they live.

Be sure to mind
Your parents kind,
    And do nothing to vex or tease them ;
But through each day
Heed what they say,
    And strive to obey and please them.
Take not in vain
God's holy name,
Do not work,
Do not play
On God's holy day,
    Nor from church stay away ;
Always bear it in mind
To be gentle and kind,
And friends you will find,
And hearts to you bind,
    I am sure I may venture to say.
And when you 're men,
Who sees you then
    I hope in you models will see,
Of *good* and *great*,
In *Church* and *State*,
    Whose lips with your lives agree.

Weston, Feb 1852

FOR MY GRAND-DAUGHTERS, M. AND L.—AN ACROSTIC.

Mary and Lily — how sweet are those names,
Allied as they are to my heart and my home;
Recalling with freshness the days that are past,
Yielding buds of sweet promise for days yet to come.

Links are these names to the chain that hath bound
In fetters my heart, to which still they lay claim;
Loved ones and lovely, still close by me found,
Years past, and time present, whose names are the same.

Enshrined in this bosom, is living one now,
Still youthful and truthful, and talented too,
Though years have elapsed since she passed from our
      view;
E'en in Summer midst roses in beauty and bloom,
She faded away, and was borne to the tomb.

Weston, March 5, 1852

FOR MY FRIEND MRS. R.

When writing to you, friend, a subject I 'd find
In which there 's both pleasure and profit combined,
And though what I 've chosen may pain in review,
Yet still there 's strange mingling of pleasure there too.
Then let us go back many years that are past,
And glance at those days *much too happy to last.*
I have seen thee, my friend, when around thy bright
      hearth
Not a seat was found vacant, but gladness and mirth
Kept high holiday there, and many a time
Were mingled in pastime my children with thine.
I 've looked in again, the destroyer had come,
And changed the whole aspect of that happy home.
He entered that dwelling, and rudely he tore
From the arms of his mother, her most cherished
      flower.

F

Thy heart seemed then broken, oh! how couldst thou
    bear
To live in this world, and thy idol not here?
Oh! heart-stricken mother, thou didst not then know
All the bitter ingredients in thy cup of woe.
The hand of thy father that cup had prepared,
Each drop needful for thee, not one could be spared.
Ere thy first wound had healed, while bleeding and sore,
Death entered again, and a fair daughter bore
From home of her childhood, to return never more.
How painful the shock, for in striking that blow
A child, parent, sister, and wife was laid low.
Thy strength seemed unequal that shock to sustain,
But death was not satiate, he soon called again,
And tears and entreaties were powerless to save
Another dear daughter from death and the grave.
Like a fair lily when droops its young head,
With little of suffering her mild spirit fled.
She was thy namesake, to her young friends most dear;
So many thy trials, so heavy to bear,
It seemed that much longer thou couldst not survive;
How much can the human heart bear and yet live.
Up to this time there had always been one

Who shared in thy trials and made them his own,
Many years his strong arm had support been to thee,
The friend of thy youth, thy kind husband was he.
He's ever been with thee in weal and in woe,
But the time's just at hand when he too must go.
The bolt fell not single, it pierced the slight form
Of a child, too fragile to weather the storm,
The summons that took her dear father away
Seemed her young heart to break, she could not here
      stay,
And now in deep slumber they side by side lay.
I have felt, my dear friend, as I've witnessed thy grief,
How inadequate language to give thee relief;
And that *real relief* could never be found
Except from the hand that inflicted the wound.
In the furnace of fire thou wert not alone,
For walking beside thee had ever been one,
The kindest of friends, though thou could'st not him
      see,
For the scales on thine eyes weighed them down heavily
Those scales have now fallen; look up, thou canst see
That look of compassion, it's fixed upon thee.

Raise thine eyes once again, see that head crowned with
    thorns;
In those feet, hands, and side, see the deep bleeding
    wounds.
You now know full well why such suffering was borne,
'T was for thee, and for me, and for every one
Who trusts in his merits and on him alone.
Thy day is just passed, 't is now evening with thee,
But the faith of the Christian is given to see
The star of bright promise, amid the dark gloom
Which shall light all thy footsteps and gild the lone
    tomb;
And at the last day mayst thou and thine stand
An *unbroken household* at Jesus' right hand.

March 27, 1852

FOR MY NIECE ANGELINE.

In the morning of life, when all things appear bright,
And far in the distance the shadows of night,
With kind parents still spared thee, and health to enjoy,
What period more fitting thy powers to employ
In the service of him, who his own life has given
To procure thee a crown and a mansion in Heaven.
As a dream that is gone at the breaking of day,
And a tale that 's soon told, so our years pass away.
"Then count that day lost, whose low setting sun
Can see from thy hand no worthy act done."
Midst the roses of life many thorns thou wilt find,
"But the cloud that is darkest, with silver is lined."
As the children of Israel were led on their way
By the bright cloud at night, and the dark cloud by day,
So the Christian is led through the straight narrow road
That brings him direct to his home and his God;

And when the last stage of life's journey is o'er,
And Jordan's dark waves can affright him no more,
When safely arrived in his own promised land,
He's permitted with Saints and with Angels to stand,
Then weighed in the balance how light will appear
All the sorrows of life, with his blissful state there.
Oh! let us by faith take a view of him now,
See the crown of bright jewels encircling his brow,
His old tattered robe swept away by the flood,
Is replaced by a new one, the gift of his Lord,
The hand of his Saviour that garment hath wrought,
It is pure stainless white, free from wrinkle and spot.
The streets that he walks in are paved with gold,
And yet it's transparent as glass we are told;
The pure river of water of life is in view,
And for healing the nations, the tree of life too.
There's no need of a candle or sun there, for night
Is excluded forever — the Lord God is their light.
But here we will stop, for no tongue can declare,
No heart may conceive what the Saints enjoy there.
And these joys may be ours — oh! how blissful the
      thought,
Ours without money, without price may be bought.

For us they 've been purchased by the Son of God,
At an infinite price — *his own precious blood*.
They wait our acceptance, may be ours if we choose,
'T is *life* to accept them, — 't is *death* to refuse.

Weston, May 15, 1852

AN ACROSTIC.

Ah! what is this life?   It's a dream, is the reply;
Like a dream that's soon ended, so life passes by.
Pursue the thought further, still there's likeness in
      each,
How constant our aim is at what we can't reach.
E'en so in a dream, we've some object in view
Unceasingly aimed at, but the thing we pursue
Still eludes our fond grasp, and yet lures us on too.

How analagous this to our waking day hours,
Unwearied our efforts, we tax all our powers;
Betimes in the morning the prize we pursue,
By the pale lamp of midnight we're seeking it too;
At all times and seasons, this *same fancied good*
Repels our advances, yet still is pursued,
Depriving us oft, of rest needful, and food.

But there's a pearl of great price, whose worth is
    untold,
It can never be purchased with silver or gold;
Great peace it confers upon all to whom given,
Ever cheering their pathway, and pointing to heaven.
Look not to this world for a prize of such worth,
Or hope *that* to obtain from this perishing earth
Whose essence is spiritual, and heavenly its birth.

Weston, June 5, 1852

G

ACROSTIC.

Even now I seem to see thee,
Lovely boy, with thy sweet smile,
Bright and beautiful as when
Reading that holy book, the while
I listened to thee, little dreaming,
Docile, gentle, pleasant child,
God who gave, *so soon would take thee*,
Even thee, so *sweet*, so *mild*.
But how merciful in chastening
Our father is — oh! bless his name.
Your little face was decked with smiles,
Dear child, just when the summons came.
Escaped from lingering sickness, thou hadst
Nought to mar thy little frame.
While ye mourn the dear departed,
Each bitter feeling disallow,

Look to heaven, ye broken hearted,

Look, and with submission bow.

In thy hour of deepest sorrow,

Never murmur, dare not blame;

God, who wounds, alone can heal thee;

Trust his power and praise his name.

Oh! may we say, *each*, every one,

"Not my will, but thine be done."

SHE SLUMBERS STILL.

On a midsummer's eve she lay down to sleep,
Wearied and toil-worn the maiden was then ;
How deep was that slumber, how quiet that rest,
'T was the sleep from which no one awakens again.

Morn returned in its freshness, and flowers that she
      loved
In beauty and fragrance were blooming around ;
The birds caroled sweetly the whole live-long day,
But that strange mystic sleep all her senses had bound.

Day followed day until summer was gone,
And autumn still found her alone and asleep ;
Stern winter soon followed, but its loud blasts and
      shrill,
Were powerless to rouse her from slumber so deep.

Again spring returns, and all nature revives,
And birds fill the groves with their music again;
But the eyes and the ears of that loved one are closed,
And on her these rich treasures are lavished in vain.

Unheeded by her the winter snow falls,
Its beautiful garment spring puts on in vain;
Many *summers* the birds her sad requiem have sung,
But to sound of sweet music she 'll ne'er wake again.

There is *but one voice* that deep slumber can break,
'T is the same one that loudly called, "Lazarus, come
      forth!"
At the sound of that voice all the dead shall arise,
And before God shall stand all the nations on earth.

Then shall this dear one, our first born, awake,
Her mortal put on immortality then;
And oh! blissful thought, that we once more may meet
In that home where 's no parting, death, sorrow, or pain.

Weston, May 29, 1852.

TO A FRIEND IN THE CITY,

FROM HER FRIEND IN THE COUNTRY

By especial request I take up my pen,
To write a few lines to my dear Mrs. N.;
And though nothing of depth she has right to expect,
Yet the *will* for the *deed* she will no doubt accept.
The task, on reflection, is a heavy one quite,
As here in the country we 've no news to write;
For what is to *us* very *new*, rich, and rare,
To you in the city is stale and thread bare.
Should I write of Hungary, Kossuth, or the Swede,
They are all out of date, antiquated indeed.
I might ask you with me the New Forest to roam,
But it 's stript of its foliage, quite leafless become;

N. P. Willis and rival have each had their day,

And of rappings and knockings there's nought new to
    say.

Yet do not mistake me, or think I would choose,

A home in the city, the country to lose;

The music of birds, with rich fruits and sweet flowers,

We all in the country lay claim to as ours.

A bird that's imprisoned, I hate to hear sing,

Let me catch its glad note as it soars on the wing;

Its carol so sweet as it's floating along,

It seems the Creator to praise in its song.

With the sweetest of poets I often exclaim,

"God made the country,"—let the pride of man claim

The town with its buildings, its spires, and its domes,

But leave us in the country our sweet quiet homes.

The scenery around us is lovely to view,

It charmed when a *child*, and at three-score charms too.

Then leave me the country with its birds, fruits, and
    flowers,

And the *town*, with its pleasures and crowds, may be
    yours.

E'en in winter the country has right to the claim
Of charms equal to summer; to be sure, not the same..
See winter, stern monarch, as borne on the gale,
He comes armed *cap-a-pie* in his white coat of mail ,
Behold what a change he hath wrought in *one* night,
He has robed the whole country in *pure spotless white.*
He fails not to visit us once every year,
But finds us *prepared for him*—meets with good cheer,
And a most cordial welcome from all of us here.
When with us he's quite civil and very polite,
In manners most courtly, and dignified quite ;
But I 'm told were he goes unexpected he 's rough,
Chills all by his presence, and savage enough.
Hark, hear how it storms! blowing high and yet higher;
But then we 've books, music, and a brilliant wood fire,
Where logs piled on logs give one warmth e'en to see ;
Oh ! these evenings in winter are charming to me.
In good keeping these logs are with wind and the hail,
Everything in the country is on a *grand scale.*
You have nought in the city I think can compare,
To the bright glowing hearth from a good *country* fire.

To be sure, now and then, one is cheered by the sight
Of wood fire in the city, but when at its height
Compared to *our fires*, Lilliputianal quite.
But here I will stop, for I think it quite time
To have done with my boasting, and finish my rhyme.

M. A. H. T. BIGELOW.

Weston, April 5, 1852

P.S. And now, my dear friend, it is certainly fair,
  Your city advantages you should compare
  With ours in the country, let me know what they
  are.

H

REPLY:

DEAR MADAM,

Many thanks for your missive so charming in verse,
So kind and descriptive, so friendly and terse;
It came opportune on a cold stormy day,
And scattered ennui and "blue devils" away;
For though in the city, where "all 's on the go,"
We often aver we feel only "so so,"
And sigh for a change — then *here* comes a letter!
What could I desire more welcome and better?
But how to reply? I 'm lost in dismay,
I cannot in rhyme my feelings portray.
The *nine* they discard me, I 'm not of *their* train,
They entreatingly beg, "I 'll ne'er woo them again;"
But I 'll brave their displeasure, and e'en write to *you*
A few lines of doggrel, then rhyming adieu.

My errors do " wink at," for hosts you 'll descry,
And spare all rebuff, and the keen critic's eye.
I appreciate all of your calm country life,
And feel you are happy as mother and wife,
Surrounded by taste, and *the friend* so refined,
Who with sterling good sense, loves the delicate mind;
Who with *you* can admire the " bird on the wing,"
With *you* welcome back the return of the spring;
Enjoying the promise of fruits and sweet flowers,
With music to cheer and beguile evening hours;
Then *long*, very long, may such hours be given —
They whisper content, and the foretaste of heaven.
I was born in the city, the city 's my home,
Yet oft in the country with pleasure I roam,
For *there*, I confess, the heart finds repose
In its pleasures and sorrows, which *here* it ne'er knows.

There no fashion, no nonsense, intrude on your walk,
But rational moments of rational talk,
Asserting that soirics, with jewels and dress,
Make a very small part of life's happiness.
Ah! this I believe, most *sincerely* I do,
And sympathize freely, most truly with you.

Now Kossuth is coming, pray what 's to be done?
No pageant to welcome, to children no fun?
Some "turn a cold shoulder," and look with disdain,
Yet many there 'll be who will follow his train
He's "sure missed a figure," and "bit his own nose,"
Ah, many the thorn he 'll find 'mid life's rose.

Then we've concerts, fine readings, museum and balls,
With disputes, and debates, in legislative halls,
Ethiopian Minstrels, Shakesperian plays;
And yet, my dear friend, I 'm told in these days,
Religion's blessed joys are most faithfully felt,
With devotion's pure prayers the proud heart to melt;
That many have turned to the straight narrow road,
Which leadeth to peace and communion with God.
To *you* this assurance a welcome will find,
A subject of vital concern to the mind.

When hither you come, do enter our door,
I 'll give you my hand, perhaps something more.
Let me urge, if inclined, to this you 'll reply,
I 'll again do my best, yes, surely I 'll try;
The fair one who brings it ought sure to inspire

Some poetical lay from Genius' sweet lyre.

But Genius repels me, she " turns a deaf ear,"

And frowns on me scornful, the year after year ;

Perhaps if I sue, in the " sere yellow leaf,"

She 'll open her heart, and yield me relief.

But wayward my pen, I must now bid adieu,

My friendship, dear madam, I offer to you,

And beg with your friends, you 'll please place my
name,

The privilege grant me of doing the same.

S. NICHOLSON.

Boston, April 16, 1852

REJOINDER TO THE FOREGOING REPLY.

Many, many thanks my friend,
For those sweet verses thou didst send,
  So good they were and witty;
And now I will confess to thee,
Mixed up with bad, much good I see
  Within the crowded city.

Boston, "with all thy faults I love
Thee still," though much I disapprove —
  See much in thee to blame;
Yet to be candid, I'll allow
Thy equal no one can me show
  From Mexico to Maine.

It is my boast, perhaps my pride,
To be to English blood allied,
 Warm in my veins it 's flowing;
And when I see the homage given
To foreign men and foreign *women*, *
 That blood with shame is glowing.

I hope when Kossuth fever 's cool
And we have put our wits to school,
 And sober senses found;
When the Hungarian 's out of sight
And shattered brains collected quite,
 We may be safe and sound.

But what simpletons, should we choose,
With nought to gain and much to loose,
 'Gainst Austria to war;
What greater folly, when we know
By doing this, we 'll get a blow
 From the ambitious Czar.

---

* By this I do not mean to include all foreigners, for some of them I consider among the very best of our population, but dancers, &c , &c

But you may not with me agree,
And I am getting warm I see,
　　So here I bid adieu
To Kossuth and to Hungary,
To Russia and to Germany,
　　And the great Emperor too.

And now my friend a word I'd say
Before I throw my pen away,
　　On subject most important;
In doing this I need not fear
I shall offend the nicest ear,
　　Or strike a note discordant.

Oh! had I true poetic fire,
With boldness would I strike the lyre
　　So loud that all might hear;
But ah! my harp is tuned so low,
Its feeble strains I full well know
　　Can reach no distant ear.

Yet I rejoice that harps on high,
And voices of sweet harmony,

Are raised to bless the name
Of Him who sits upon the throne,
Rejoicing over souls new born,
　　Who soon will join with them,
Eternally His name to adore
Who died, yet lives forevermore.

Weston, May 8, 1852.

I

TO MY FRIEND MR. J ELLIS.

To thee, the guardian of my youthful days,
Fain would I pay some tribute of respect,
And though it falls far short of thy deseit,
The *will* to do thee justice thou 'lt accept.

As I recall the days of former years,
Thy many acts of kindness bring to mind,
Tears fill my eyes, in thee I 've ever found
A friend most faithful, uniformly kind.

Thou art the earliest friend of mine that 's left —
The rest have long departed, every one ;
They 've long years since the debt of nature paid,
But thou remainest still, and thou alone.

The snow of four score winters thou has seen,
And life's long pilgrimage may soon be o'er ;
Respected, loved, and happy hast thou been,

With ample means to relieve the suffering poor,
Thou ever hadst the will, as well as power.

Temperate in habit, and of temper even,
Calm and unruffled as the peaceful lake,
To thee the satisfaction has been given
Much to enjoy, and others happy make.

And when thy days on earth shall all be past,
And thou before the Saviour's bar appear,
Mayst thou be found clothed in his righteousness
And from his lips the joyful sentence hear —

" Well done, thou good and faithful servant, thou
Hast over few things faithful been, and now
I 'll make thee ruler over many things,
And place a crown of glory on thy brow."

Such will be thy reward, my friend, and mine,
If trusting in Christ's merits, *not our own*,
We at the last great day in him be found ;
He is the ark of safety — *He alone.*

Weston, April 24, 1852

A PASTORAL.

Oh! tell me ye shepherds, tell me I pray,
Have you seen the fair Jessie pass by this way?
You ne'er could forget her, if once you had seen,
She's fair as the morning, she moves like a Queen.

My sheep are neglected, my crook's thrown aside,
In pursuit of dear Jessie, sweet Jessie, my bride;
I hear nothing of her, no tidings can glean,
To *see* is to *know* her, she moves like a Queen.

Say, have you seen her? oh, pity my grief!
Speak *quick*, and impart me the needful relief;
You cannot forget her, if once you have seen,
She's lovely as Venus, she moves like a Queen.

Have you not seen her ? — then listen I pray,
Oh! listen to what a poor shepherd can say
In the praise of one ne'er so lovely was seen ;
She 's youthful as Hebe, she moves like a Queen.

She 's fair as the Spring in the mild month of May,
She 's brilliant as June decked in flowerets so gay ;
You ne'er could forget her if once you had seen,
She 's charming as Flora, she moves like a Queen.

Oh! tell me not Damon, that yours can compare
To Jessie, sweet Jessie, with beauty so rare ;
With a face of such sweetness, so modest a mien,
She 's like morn in its freshness, she moves like a Queen

You tell me your Sylvia is beautiful quite ;
She may be, when Jessie is kept out of sight,
She is not to be mentioned with Jessie, I ween,
Her voice is sweet music, she moves like a Queen.

Then name not your Sylvia with Jessie I pray,
'Tis comparing dark night with the fair light of day ;
Sylvia's movements are clumsy, and awkwardly seen,
But Jessie is graceful, she moves like a Queen.

Menalaus' fair wife, for beauty far famed,
By the side of my Jessie is not to be named,
Paris ne'er had woo'd Helen, if Jessie he'd seen,
She's chaste as Diana, she moves like a Queen.

Oh! aid me, do aid me, ye shepherds, I pray!
The time is fast flying, no longer I'll stay;
You cannot mistake her, there's none like her seen,
She's lovely as Venus, she moves like a Queen.

Do help me to find her, I'm wild with affright,
The day passes swiftly, it soon will be night;
There's none to compare with her, none like her seen,
More lovely than Venus, she moves like a Queen.

THE JESSAMINE.

EDDIE TO JESSIE

There are many flowers famous for fragrance and hue,
Sweet Roses and Lilies, Geraniums too,
And though decked in gay colors they look very fine,
They are not to my fancy like *sweet Jessie mine.*

FOR THE S. S. CONCERT,

IN THE WAYLAND ORTHODOX CHURCH

Feed my lambs! the Saviour said,
'Near two thousand years ago,
If we truly love the Lord,
By obedience, love we 'll show.

What was said to Peter then,
In that distant age and clime,
Sure is binding on us now,
Here and to the end of time.

If our Shepherd then we love,
His commandments we 'll obey,
Let us true disciples prove,
Feed his lambs as best we may.

Twice twelve years have passed this day,*
Since our Sabbath School commenced;
Countless lessons have been learned,
Much instruction been dispensed.

Let us up and doing be,
Sow the seed all times and hours;
Cast our bread on water even,
Tax with vigor all our powers.

May the teachers now engaged,
Courage take, and persevere,
They'll not fail of their reward,
Though they may not meet it here.

God is faithful, who hath said,
(Let the thought allay your fears,)
"They with joy shall surely reap,
Who have sown in prayers and tears."

---

* June 13, 1852

Then sow the seed with prayers and tears,
Never doubt, but faithful be,
Though thou reapest not for years,
A rich harvest thou wilt see.

Happy faces now we miss,
Who were wont these seats to fill;
Loved and lovely passed away,
Yet they're fresh in memory still.

Soon their earthly race was run,
In the morning called away;
Others soon may follow them,
May all hear the Saviour say,

" Well done, faithful servant, thou
Hast o'er few things faithful been,
I will make the ruler now
Over many — enter in."

FEED MY LAMBS.

Just before the bright cloud the Saviour received,
When about to return to his father in Heaven;
His mission accomplished, his work on earth done,
'T was then that this parting injunction was given :

" Feed my lambs!" this was said to one of the twelve,
Whom he called to be with him while sojourning here;
" Feed my lambs'" Oh, what love was evinced by those
        words,
What tender compassion, what fatherly care.

Three times at this meeting the question was asked,
" Simon, son of Jonas, lovest thou me?"
And though grieved, yet how truly could Peter reply,
" Lord thou knowest all things, thou know'st I love
        thee."

Thrice this same Peter his Lord had denied,
And had he not reason reproaches to fear?
Oh, no! for his Saviour had all this forgiven,
He saw his repentance, he knew it sincere

That disciple soon followed his Lord whom he loved,
And many long ages have since passed away;
But the parting command still remains in full force,
And will ever remain so till time's latest day.

Many wolves in sheep's clothing are still to be found,
Whom Satan fails not to instruct and employ;
They enter the fold, and with most specious wiles,
Seek the young of the flock to ensnare and destroy.

And shall we dare call ourselves followers of Christ,
And yet his known precepts presume to evade?
Ah! stop and reflect, what's the test that's required?
" If ye love me, keep my commandments," he said.

June 26, 1852

"GOD IS LOVE."

Come blest Spirit from above,
Come and fill my heart with love;
Love to God, and love to man,
Love to do the good I can;
Love to high, and love to low,
Love to friend, and love to foe.
Love to rich, and love to poor,
Love to beggar at my door.
Love to young, and love to old,
Love to hardened heart and cold.
Love, true love, my heart within
For the sinner, *not the sin ;*
Love to holy Sabbath day,
Love to meditate and pray,
Love for love, for *hatred* even ;
Love like this, is born of Heaven.

TO MY FRIEND MRS. LLOYD.

My very dear friend
Should never depend
Upon anything clever or witty,
From a poor country wight
When attempting to write,
To one in your far famous city.
Indeed I 'm inclined,
To fear that you 'll find
These lines heavy, and quite out of joint;
And now I declare,
It 's no more than fair,
Should this prove a dull letter,
That you write me a better;
And something that 's quite to the point.
This having premised
As at present advised,

I 'll indulge in the thoughts that incline,
Not with curious eye
The dim future to spy,
But glance backward to "Auld Lang Syne."
If I recollect right,
It was a cold day quite,
And not far from night
When *the Boarding School famous* I entered.
Now what could I do?
Scarce above my own shoe
Did I dare take a view,
Or to speak, or e'en move hardly ventured.
At this school I remained
Till supposed to have gained
Education quite good and sufficient;
But one in those days,
Thought deserving of praise,
Would in these, be deemed very deficient.
And here we will try
Before the mind's eye,
To bring forward a few of that household;
There were the witty,
Also the pretty,

But some very plain,
Not a few very vain,
And among them the phlegmatic and cold.
Though it seems out of place
I will here find a space
For some few in the lower department;
Sure this must be right,
They contributed quite
To our comfort, in their humble department.
Here's Lydia and Polly,
And Peter the jolly,
With teeth white as ivory
And cheeks black as ebony,
So from Africa doubtless was he;
But we'll ascend from below,
And see entering just now
With a Parisian bow
And all in a glow
Gay Monsieur Pichon,
And French teacher Faucon;
Also V ——, the Musician,
And B ——, Mathematician.
Monsieur Laboltierre,

So brisk and debonnair
Had also been there;
And there's Eggleston fair,
With whom none might compare.
Miss W ——, romantic,
Miss F ——, transatlantic,
And of others a score you might see.
But here I propose
The long list to close,
With addition of only one name;
Amidst the gay throng
Was one lovely and young,
Who brought sunshine wherever she came.
She had light brown hair,
Was graceful and fair,
Of children many
Youngest of any,
And Margaret this maiden they call;
A sweet smile she had
That round her lips played,
And with eyes bright and blue
She'd a heart warm and true
And disposition affectionate withal.

One advantage she 'll allow
That I have over her now,
The same in our youthful days, when
On our studies intent
Over school desk we bent,
Her Senior I always have been.
How like to a dream
Do those days to me seem,
When with others preparing to enter
On the world's great stage,
And with light heart engage
Our part in the drama to venture.
Of that school there 's not one
Except thee alone,
Whom now living as friend I can claim;
Some have departed,
Some are false hearted,
And their friendship exists but in name.
But that friendship 's long lived
That forty years has survived,
And may we not hope 't will endure,
When in flames of fire
This earth will expire,
And old time shall itself be no more.

July 12, 1852

L

ESCAPE OF THE ISRAELITES,

AND DESTRUCTION OF PHARAOH

Ah! short-sighted monarch, dost thou think to pursue
The Israel of God, and recapture them too ?
Hast thou so soon forgotten the plagues on thee sent,
Or so hardened thy heart that thou can'st not relent ?
Then make ready thy chariots, a long way they 'll reach;
Thou hast six hundred chosen, a captain to each.
Now after them *hasten*, no time 's to be lost,
That God worketh for them, thou 'st felt to thy cost.
Speed thee then, speed thee, thou 'lt soon them o'ertake,
Thou hast so overtasked them they 're powerless and
      weak.
Ah! weak and defenceless they truly appear,
But the Lord is their rock, they are his special care.
See that pillar that 's leading them all on their way,
It 's a bright cloud by night and a dark cloud by day ;

And now by the Red Sea behold they encamp,

But *hark!* what's that sound, it's the war horse's tramp.

Look up, see thy enemy close by thee now,

The sea lies before thee, ah! what canst thou do?

Moses bids them go forward at God's command,

When the waters divide, and they walk on dry land;

And the cloud that to Egypt is darkness all night,

To the children of Israel, is a bright shining light.

And now have the Hebrews all safely passed through

The Red Sea, which Pharaoh assaying to do

Is destroyed with his host; every one of them drowned,

Not a man saved alive, not a *single man found*

To return to lone Egypt, the sad news to bear

To the widows and orphans made desolate there.

But list! hear the rescued their glad voices raise,

And to timbrel and dance add the sweet song of praise,

For Pharaoh hath perished beneath the dark sea,

And the long enslaved Hebrews are happy and free.

July 14, 1852

HYMN,

SUNG AT THE ORDINATION OF THE REV HENRY ALLEN

We meet to-day as ne'er before,
To greet a pastor of our choice,
Without a single jarring note,
And without one dissenting voice.

Oh thou who art enthroned on high,
Before whom holy angels bow,
Be pleased to hear us when we sing,
Accept the praises offered now..

Let no one present, dare to give,
The service of the lip alone;
Or think if they the heart withhold,
'Twill find acceptance at thy throne.

But with united heart and voice,
A grateful tribute we would raise;
Oh bless us all assembled now,
Help us to pray, and help to praise.

Thou great Immanuel, who didst lead
Thy Israel all the desert through;
Like them we 're weak and helpless quite,
Oh! condescend to lead *us* too.

And when our Shepherd with his flock
Before thy throne shall re-appear,
May every one acceptance find,
And ceaseless praises offer there.

Sept 1852

MARGARET'S REMEMBRANCE OF LIGHTFOOT.

My beautiful steed,
'T is painful indeed
To think we are parted forever;
That on no sunny day,
With light spirits and gay,
Over hills far away,
We shall joyously travel together.

Thy soft glossy mane
I shall ne'er see again,
Nor thy proudly arched neck 'gain behold;
Nor admire *that* in thee,
Which so seldom we see,
A kind, gentle spirit, yet bold.

Thou wert pleasant indeed
My darling grey steed,
" In my mind's eye " thou 'rt beautiful still ,
For when thou wert old
Thy heart grew not cold,
Its warm current time never could chill.

Not a stone marks the spot
Where they laid thee, Lightfoot,
And no fence to enclose thee around ,
But what if there 's not,
Deep engraved on my heart
Thy loved image may ever be found.

"THE CLOUDS RETURN AFTER THE RAIN."

Dark and yet darker my day's clouded o'er;
Are its bright joys all fled, and its sunshine no more?
I look to the skies for the bright bow in vain,
For constantly "clouds return after the rain."

Must it always be thus, peace banished forever,
And joy to this sad heart returned again never?
I long for the rest that I cannot obtain,
For the clouds, so much dreaded, return after rain.

Is there not in this wide world one spot that is blessed
With exemption from suffering, where one may find
     rest;
Where sickness and sorrow no entrance can gain,
And the clouds do not return after the rain?

Ah! deceive not thyself by a vain hope like this,
Nor expect in this world to enjoy lasting peace:
But bow with submission to God's holy will,
For the hand that afflicts is thy kind Father's still

If my days are dark here, there are brighter above,
In those pure realms of light, peace, joy, and of love,
Where the air is all balm, and the skies ever fair,
And the river of life, clear as crystal flows there.

There also, for healing the nations, are found
The leaves of the tree on which rich fruits abound;
There is no need of candle, for God is their light,
There never is darkness, for " *there* is no night."

Oh! may I there find, when this brief life is past,
By my Saviour prepared, a sweet home at last;
Where sin never enters, death, sorrow, nor care,
And clouds are not feared, for it never rains there.

August 19, 1852

M

THE NOCTURNAL VISIT.

Lo the curtains of night around Palestine fall,
And Jerusalem's streets into darkness are thrown ;
The late busy hum of men's voices is hushed,
And the city is clad in dark livery alone.

But see through the dimness that half opened door,
And slowly emerging a figure behold ;
A quick, furtive glance he has thrown all around,
For what is he thirsting, for blood, or for gold ?

Stealthily, fearfully, onward he moves,
So light are his footsteps you scarce hear their tread ;
Yet no midnight robber, no murderer is he,
Then why dread recognition — of man why afraid ?

Let us follow his footsteps and learn where he goes;
And now at the door of a house see him stand;
But why wait so long ere admittance he seeks,
In attempting to knock, why trembles that hand?

He has come to the fountain of light and of life,
Before whom ne'er suppliant sued humbly in vain;
He has come for the knowledge that alone maketh rich,
And without which we're poor, though the whole world
     we gain.

He has come to learn wisdom of that lowly one,
Who spake as " never man spake " it was said;
And who, though so poor and despised among men,
Is the whole world's Sustainer, creation's great Head.

But list to the words of the Saviour of men,
" Verily, verily I say unto thee,
That no man, except he be born again,
Is permitted the kingdom of heaven to see."

How humbling to pride were these words of our Lord,
What fears in his guest they serve to awaken,

Though a ruler of Jews, he was yet in his sins ;
The first step towards heaven he never had taken.

Ah! Nicodemus, how many like thee,
Would perceive all their boasted religion was vain,
Could they meet but his glance who " searcheth the
      heart,
And trieth the reins of the children of men."

                          Sept 9, 1852

SOVEREIGNTY OF GOD AND FREE AGENCY OF MAN.

Thou art a perfect Sovereign, oh my God!
And I rejoice to think that thou art so;
That all events are under thy control,
And that thou knowest all I think and do.
- But some may ask, "then why am I to blame
Because I sin, if God hath made me thus?"
Stop, stop, my friend, God tempteth not to sin,
Thou dost it of thy own free will and choice.
Though God is Sovereign, we free agents are,
Accountable to him for all we do,
Feel, think, or say; and at the last great day,
A most exact account must render too.

With this conclusion be thou satisfied —
For all who will accept him, Christ hath died

Sept 19, 1852

God is a Sovereign, man free agent too ;
How these to reconcile I do not know :
But *this* I know, if *lost,* the blame is *mine,*
If saved, the *praise,* oh God ! be *only thine.*

AUTUMN AND SUNSET.

Hail, sober Autumn! thee I love,
Thy healthful breeze and clear blue sky;
And *more* than flowers of Spring admire
Thy falling leaves of richer dye.

'T was even thus when life was young,
I welcomed Autumn with delight;
Although I knew that with it came
The shorter day and lengthened night.

Let others pass October by,
Or dreary call its hours, or chill;
Let poets always sing of Spring,
My praise shall be of Autumn still.

And I have loved the setting sun,
E'en than his rising beams more dear;
'T is fitting time for serious thought,
It is an hour for solemn prayer.

Before the evening closes in,
Or night's dark curtains round us fall,
See how o'er tree, and spire, and hill,
That setting sun illumines all.

So when my earthly race is run,
When called to bid this world adieu,
Like yonder cloudless orb I see,
May *my* sun set in glory too.

O.t 8, 1852

"MY TIMES ARE IN THY HAND."

My times are in thy hand, my God!
And I rejoice that they are so;
My times are in thy hand, my God,
Whether it be for weal or woe.

My times are in thy hand, I know;
And if I 'm washed in Jesus' blood,
Though dark my pathway here below,
It leads directly up to God.

Since all thy children chastening need,
And all *so called* must feel the rod,
Why for exemption should I plead,
For am I not thy child, my God?

N

Ah why go mourning all the day,
Or why should I from trials shrink?
Though much of sorrow 's in my cup,
The cup that I am called to drink.

'T is needful medicine I know,
By the most skilful hand prepared,
Strictly proportioned to my wants,
There 's *not a drop* that can be spared.

Then why desponding, oh my soul,
Because of trials here below?
They 're all appointed by my God,
My times are in thy hand, I know.

Jan 18, 1853

NOVEMBER.

Remember the poor, in the dark chilly day,
When November's loud winds are fierce blowing;
Remember the poor, at thy plentiful board,
When the fire on thy bright hearth is glowing.

Remember the poor in yon damp dismal shed,
Without food, fire, or clothing to warm them;
And not like the Priest or the Levite pass by,
But Samaritan like stop and cheer them.

Remember the slave, the poor down trodden slave,
And do all in thy power to relieve him;
And when from oppression he strives to be free,
Do thou open thy gate to receive him.

For what saith the Lord is thy duty to such,
"To his master thou shalt not return him," *
But give him a home near thy own if he likes,
And be sure not to vex or oppress him.

When parents or children or brethren you meet,
In our happy New England and free,
Then remember the slave, the heart broken slave,
For thy brother, *thy brother* is he.

Remember him also when prayer for thyself,
In affliction's dark hour doth ascend;
And when crying to God the father of all,
Let *his* wants with *thine own* kindly blend.

And at the last day, when the rich and the poor
Shall alike by the *Judge* be regarded;
When master and slave shall appear before God,
And a sentence impartial awarded, —

* See Deuteronomy, 23   15 16

The cup of cold water He will not forget,
But with other good acts bring to mind;
"When naked ye clothed me, when hungry ye fed,"
Will be uttered in accents most kind.

But when, blessed Saviour, ah when was the time,
That we fed, clothed, or visited thee?
"Such acts," He replies, "to my poor brethren done,
I consider as done unto me."

Nov 1852

WINTER.

His thundering car
Is heard from afar,
And his trumpet notes sound
All the country around;
Stop your ears as you will,
That loud blast and shrill
Is heard by you still.
Borne along by the gale,
In his frost coat of mail,
Midst snow, sleet, and hail,
He comes without fail,
And drives all before him,
Though men beg and implore him
Just to let them take breath,
Or he 'll drive them to death.

But he comes in great state,
And for none will he wait,
Though he sees their distress
Yet he spares them no less,
For the cold stiff limb
Is nothing to him;
And o'er countless blue noses,
His hard heart he closes.
His own children fear him
And dare not come near him;
E'en his favorite child *
Has been known to run wild
At his too near approach,
Her fear of him such,
And to shriek and to howl
And return scowl for scowl.
Indeed few dare him face,
And *all* shun his embrace;
For though pleasant his smile,
Yet one thinks all the while

---

* Spring

Of that terrible frown,
Which the hardiest clown,
Though a stout hearted man,
Will avoid if he can.
And though many maintain
That he gives needless pain,
I confess I admire
This venerable sire.
True his language is harsh,
And his conduct oft rash,
And we know well enough,
That his manners are rough ;
Yet still in the main,
We 've no right to complain,
For if we prepare for him,
And show that we care for him,
We may in him find
A true friend and kind.
With us he will stay
Three months to a day,
So let us prepare
The snug elbow chair,
Which placed by the fire

May comfort impart
And cheer his old heart.
Though he seems so unkind,
Yet always you 'll find
That his cold heart will warm,
And he 'll do you no harm
If your *own* can but *feel*
For your poor neighbor's weal;
And with pity o'erflowing,
Your free alms bestowing,
Never closing your door
On the suffering poor;
But clothe, feed, and warm them,
And see that none harm them.
E'en to others just do
As you 'd wish them by you.
Let 's adopt but this plan,
To do good when we can,
And the dark stormy day
Will full quick pass away,
And we never complain
Of cold weather again,
Or of tedious long hours,
That are spent within doors;

o

For when winter winds blow,
And we 're hedged up by snow,
We shall find full employment,
And lack no enjoyment.
Thus prepared, let him come,
He will find us at home;
Bring wind, hail, or snow,
Blow high, or blow low,
We 're prepared for him now.
Then come winter, come,
You 'll find us at home.

Nov 5, 1852

* * * * * *

There is within this heart of mine,
An aching void earth ne'er can fill;
I 've tried its joys, its friendships proved,
But felt that aching void there *still.*

Thy love alone, my Saviour God,
True satisfaction can impart,
Can fill this aching void I feel,
And give contentment to my heart.

Oh! cheer me by thy presence, Lord,
Increase my faith an hundred fold,
Be *thy name* on my forehead found,
Mine in thy book of life enrolled.

Dec 19, 1852

Forever closed that dark blue eye,
Full and expressive, pensive too;
Thy light brown hair, and face so fair,
And graceful form are hid from view.

LIFE'S CHANGES.

A fair young girl was to the altar led
By him she loved, the chosen of her heart;
And words of solemn import there were said,
And mutual vows were pledged till death should part.

But life was young, and death a great way off,
At least it seemed so then, on that bright morn;
And they no doubt, expected years of bliss,
And in their path the rose without a thorn.

Cherished from infancy with tenderest care,
A precious only daughter was the bride,
And when that young protector's arm she took,
She for the first time left her parents' side.

With all a woman's tender, trustful heart,
She gave herself away to him she loved;
Why should she not, was he not all her own,
A choice by friends and parents too approved?

How rapidly with him the days now fly,
With *him* the partner of her future life;
Happy and joyous as a child she'd been,
Happy as daughter, *happier still as wife*

But ere eight months in quick succession passed,
One to each human heart a dreaded foe,
Entered her house, and by a single stroke,
Blasted her hopes, and laid her idol low.

Three months of bitter anguish was endured,
But hope again revived, and she was blest,
When pressing to her heart a darling child,
Whose little head she pillowed on her breast.

Not long is she permitted to enjoy,
This sweetest bud of promise to her given;
Short as an angel's visit was its stay,

Ah, what a contrast one short year presents!
Replete with happiness — replete with woe;
In that brief space, a maiden called, and wife,
Widow and mother written — childless too.

Surely my friend, I need not say to thee,
Look not to earth for what it can't bestow;
'T is at the best a frail and brittle reed,
Which trusting for support, will pierce thee through.

Then let us look above this fleeting earth,
To heaven and heavenly joys direct our eyes;
No lasting happiness this world affords —
" He builds too low who builds below the skies."

Weston, Dec. 1, 1852

LINES.

" They will not frame their doings to turn unto their God   IIosea, 5 4 "

I would frame all my doings to please thee, my God!
'T is from thee all my mercies proceed ;
I would frame all my doings to serve thee, my God!
For thy service is freedom indeed.

I would frame all my doings to please thee, my God!
But how feeble my best efforts are ;
Ah! how needful for me is thy chastening rod,
And a proof of thy fatherly care.

I would frame all my doings to serve thee, my God!
But my goodness extends not to thee,
And when on well doing I 'm fully intent,
Alas! evil is present with me.

My Creator, Preserver, Redeemer and King,
I would tax all my powers to obey;
But to Him let me look for the help that I need,
Who is the life, the light, and the way.

Weston, Jan 21 1853

"TAKE NO THOUGHT FOR THE MORROW."

Take no thought for the morrow, the Saviour hath said,
And he spake as ne'er man spake before,
"He carried our sorrows," "was acquainted with grief,"
And knew well what the heart could endure.

Let the morrow take care for the things of itself,
And not by its weight crush thee down,
Sufficient to-day is the evil thereof,
Let the ills of to-morrow alone

Neither boast of to-morrow, for what is thy life,
But a vapor that floateth away;
Like a *tale* quickly told, or a *dream* of the night,
That departs at the breaking of day.

P

Be not like the man who once said in his heart,
" I have goods that are laid by for years , "
But scarce had he planned how they best might be
      stored,
When he dies and leaves all to his heirs.

Neither *dread* then, nor *boast* of to-morrow, my soul,
But make most of the time that's now given ;
Be the ground well prepared, with good seed sown
      thereon,
And 't will yield a rich harvest in heaven.

Jan 24, 1853

REMINISCENCES OF THE DEPARTED.

His mission soon accomplished,
His race on earth soon run,
He passed to realms of glory,
Above the rising sun.

So beautiful that infant,
When in death's arms he lay;
It seemed like peaceful slumber,
That morn might chase away.

But morning light was powerless,
Those eyelids to unclose;
And sunshine saw and left him,
In undisturbed repose.

The light of those blue orbs
That drank the sunbeams in,
Now yields to night, and darkness
Holds undisputed reign.

That little form so graceful,
The light brown chestnut hair;
Those half formed words when uttered,
That face so sweet and fair;

All, all his ways so winning,
Were impotent to save
His life, when called to yield it
By *Him that* life who gave.

So soon his voyage ended,
The passage home so short,
Before he knew of evil,
He entered safe the port.

Since thee, my child, I saw,
Long years have passed away;
Thy mother's hair then brown,
Now 's intermixed with gray.

Another link 's been broken,
By death's relentless hand ;
A daughter has been taken,
The eldest of the band.

Thy little lamp of life,
Was put out in a day ;
But *hers* was years expiring,
By slow yet sure decay.

But *one* short year of life,
Was all allotted thee ;
But she, thy eldest sister,
Was *many* years spared me.

And though long since we parted,
On earth to meet no more ;
I 'd think of thee as children
" Not *lost*, but gone before."

Feb 20, 1853

"LET ME DIE THE DEATH OF THE RIGHTEOUS.

By the river Euphrates the prophet abode,
To whom Balak his messengers sent,
Entreating his presence and curses on those
Who on Moab's destruction were bent.

By hundreds of thousands they're marching along,
And by Moses, God's servant, they're led;
The rock for their thirst, cooling water supplies,
And with bread from the skies are they fed.

They are felling the nations like trees on their way,
And their power there is none can resist;
" Come, curse me this people, oh! Balaam, I pray,
For he whom *thou* cursest is curst."

With rich bribes in their hands have these messengers
      come,
Both from Moab and Midian are they;
Desiring the Prophet with them would return,
And this without any delay.

But the men are requested to stop over night,
That the will of the Lord he may learn,
And then if by Him he's permitted to go,
He'll accompany them on their return.

Now when earth her dark mantle of night had put on,
And men's eyes in deep slumber were sealed;
In that solemn hour was the voice of God heard,
And his will to the Prophet revealed.

" Thou shalt not 'go with them!'" distinctly was said,
" Nor to curse the Lord's people presume;"
So the Princes of Moab returned as they came,
And left Balaam reluctant at home.

Again unto Balaam were messages sent,
More in number, in *rank higher still,*

With the promise if Balak's request he would grant,
He may ask and receive what he will.

But Balaam declared that if Balak would give
Him his house full of silver and gold,
The word of the Lord he could *not* go beyond,
To do *more* or do less than he 's told.

Still the bait was quite tempting, and Balaam was
    weak,
And wicked he certainly proved ;
E'en the Ass that he rode, *that* man's conduct
    condemned,
Who the gains of unrighteousness loved.

In the country of Moab at length he arrives,
And King Balak hath met face to face,
Who requests that with him a high hill he 'd ascend,
And the Israelites curse from that place.

Three times seven altars were raised to the Lord,
And three times was the sacrifice made ;

But the curse was withheld, for whom *God* pronounced
  blest,
Even *Balaam* to *curse* was afraid.

Poor Balaam, thy case is a hard one indeed ;
Like a house that 's divided thou art ;
Both thy Maker and Mammon thou gladly would'st
  serve,
But the former requires thy whole heart.

" Let me die the death of the righteous," say'st thou,
" And my last end like his let it be ; "
But if like the righteous *unwilling to live*,
Never hope like the righteous to die.

March 24, 1853

Q

* * * * * *

Though life is young, and spirits gay,
And hope thy fond heart cheers;
Though friends are kind, and health is firm,
And death *far off* appears,

Yet think not happiness like this,
Is destined long to last;
For ere to-morrow morn, perhaps,
Thy sky may be o'ercast.

Ah! let not pleasure blind thy eyes,
Or flattery lure thy heart,
But in the morning of thy life,
Secure the better part.

March 29, 1853

THE GREAT PHYSICIAN.

"And as Moses lifted up the serpent in the wilderness, even so must the Son of man be lifted up

"That whosoever believeth in Him should not perish but have eternal life'

St John, 3 14, 15

What means that cry of anguish,
That strikes the distant ear ;
The loud and piercing wailing,
In desert wilds we hear ?

From Israel's camp it cometh,
For Israel hath rebelled ;
And these are cries of anguish,
By wrath of God impelled.

It is no common sorrow,
Extorts that bitter groan ;
'T is from the broken hearted,
And caused by sin alone.

Lo ! in the far off desert,
Upon that tented ground,
Are many hundred thousands
Of weary travellers found

In desert of Arabia,
Near forty years they roam,
And soon they are to enter
"Canaan then happy home."

But come with me and visit
A people so distressed ;
They are the seed that Jacob
When dying pronounced blessed.

We 'll draw aside the curtain
Of tent that 's nearest by,
Ah ! what a mournful picture
For stranger's curious eye.

See on that couch reclining,
A young and lovely girl,
With brow and neck half shaded,
By many a clustering curl.

She was an only daughter,
Nurtured with tenderest care ;
The idol of her parents,
And fairest of the fair.

In bloom of youth and beauty,
But yesterday she shone, ·
And her fond parents thought her
A mine of wealth unknown.

She seems like one that sleepeth,
But there's no sign of breath ;
And coil'd 'neath her arm a serpent,
Whose bite is *certain death*

Yet not alone the mourners
In this sad tent are found ;
Shriek after shriek is echoed
For many miles around.

The mother, too, is bitten,
With infant in her arms ;
And sire, in strength of manhood ;
And bride, with all her charms.

But see on pole suspended,
A serpent now appears ,
And hark ! what blissful tidings
Salute the mourner's ears.

For every one that 's bitten,
A remedy is found ;
However bad the case is,
However deep the wound.

If but *one spark* remaineth
Of life in any soul,
Just look upon this serpent,
That look will make thee whole.

But there 's a wound that 's deeper
Than fiery serpent gave ;
And bite that 's *doubly* fatal,
It kills beyond the grave.

And there 's a great physician,
That e'en *this wound* may cure ;
And those to him applying,
May life and health secure.

The broken heart he healeth,
He cures the sin-sick soul;
And all who will behold him,
May *look* and be made whole

"I am the way!" he crieth;
"And all who will may come,
I'll pardon their transgression,
And safe conduct them home.

"To cleanse from all pollution,
My blood doth freely flow,
And sins, though red as scarlet,
Shall be as white as snow.

"Thy ransom to pay for thee,
E'en my own life it cost,
And he such love that slighteth,
Forever shall be lost."

April 14, 1853.

TO MY NIECE, MRS. M. A. CALDWELL.

When days are dark and spirits low,
And hope desponding stands,
What comfort these few words bestow,
" My times are in thy hands."
That thought should every fear allay,
And every cloud dispel ,
For we are in the hands of *One*
Who " doeth all things well."

He clothes the lily of the field,
Paints the gay tulip's leaf,
Hears the young ravens when they cry,
And hastes to their relief.
That little sparrow in thy path,
He noticed when it fell ;
Numbereth the hairs upon thy head,
And " doeth all things well."

Then say not when with cares oppressed,
He hath forsaken me;
For had thy father loved thee less,
Would he so chasten thee?
A friend he takes, a Husband too,
A Child, with him to dwell;
Selects the day, the place, the hour —
" He doeth all things well."

His power is *heard* when thunders roll,
Felt when the cold wind blows,
Seen in the vivid lightning's flash,
And in the blushing rose.
He cares for monarch on his throne,
For hermit in his cell,
For sailor on the mighty deep —
" He doeth all things well."

He raiseth one to high estate,
He brings another low;
This year an empire doth create
The *next* may overthrow.

What he may plan for you or me,
While here on earth we dwell,
We know not — but of this I 'm sure,
" He doeth all things well "

Weston, April 18, 1853

THE MORNING DRIVE.

FOR MY DAUGHTER MARGARET

Very like to a dream,
Doth the time to me seem,
When with thee a young girl by my side,
One of summer's fine days,
In a one pony chaise,
We commenced in the morning our ride.

By the pine grove and nook,
Over bridge and through brook,
Quite at random we drove without fear;
While the birds of the grove,
In sweet harmony strove,
By their concert of music to cheer.

With none to molest us,

No home cares to press us,

Farther onward, and onward we roam,

But at length the skies lower,

And unhoped for the shower

Finds us many miles distant from home

Even so is life's day,

Like a fair morn in May,

With hope's bright bow of promise it cheers,

But long before night,

The sun that so bright

In the morning had shone, disappears.

Do not then I entreat,

My beloved Margaret,

Be content with this world for thy portion;

Let ambition soar *higher*,

E'en *above* earth aspire,

And to God give thy heart's true devotion.

April 29, 1853

REPLY TO A TOAST,

SENT BY MR W TO THE LADIES OF WAYLAND, AT THEIR FAIR

HELD ON MAY-DAY

Many, *many* kind thanks from the Waylandeis fair,
Who are sorry, quite sorry you could not be there,
To receive their warm greeting, partake of their cheer,
And repaid by their smiles for your wishes sincere
That health and content may your footsteps attend,
Believe me, dear sir, is the wish of your friend.

May 2, 1853

TO MR. C. R.

FOR MANY YEARS DEPRIVED OF SIGHT.

They say the sun is shining
In all his splendor now,
And clouds in graceful drapery,
Are sailing to an fro.

That birds of brilliant plumage,
Are soaring on the wing,
Exulting in the daylight,
Rejoicing as they sing.

They tell me too that roses,
E'en in *my* pathway lie;
And decked in rich apparel,
Attract the passers by.

They say the sun when setting,
Is glorious to behold;
And sheds on all at parting,
A radiant crown of gold.

And then the night's pale empress,
With all her glittering train,
The vacant throne ascending,
Resumes her peaceful reign.

That she in queenly beauty,
Subdued yet silvery light,
Makes scarcely less enchanting
Than day, the sober night.

But sights like these so cheering,
Alas, I cannot see!
The daylight and the darkness
Are both alike to me.

Yet there's a world above us,
So beautiful and fair,
That nothing here can equal,

There, in a blaze of glory,
Amidst a countless throng,
The Saviour smiles complacent,
While listening to their song.

Ten thousand times ten thousand,
Their cheerful voices raise,
While golden harps in harmony
Are tuned to sound the praise

Of Him the blest deliverer,
Who conquered when he fell,
The man of many sorrows,
The *Great Immanuel.*

But stop — I dare not venture
Too far on holy ground;
Its *heights* are too exalted,
Its *depths* are too profound.

Yet may I be permitted,
When this brief life is past,
The hope in yon bright heaven,
To find my home at last

When cleansed from all pollution,
From sin and sorrow free,
I, with unclouded vision,
My Saviour God may see.

Brooklyn, May, 1853

S

TO MY MISSIONARY FRIENDS

.

MR AND MRS I G LLISS

Why, dear friends, oh ' tell us wherefore
You 're so anxious to be gone,
Is the country late adopted
Dearer to you than your own ?

Have you found a father, mother,
In that distant clime to love,
Or a sister, friend, or brother,
Better than the long-tried prove ?

" Oh, no ' believe us, no such motives
Prompt us to tempt old ocean's wave ;
We go among the poor benighted,
Perhaps to find an early grave.

"Ah! you know not half our anguish—
 Only those who *feel* can tell—
When we think of the sad parting,
 And that solemn word—farewell.

" But while lingering, souls are dying,
 Souls that Jesus came to save,
And of such a priceless value,
 That for them his life he gave.

" Trials great no doubt await us
 In that distant home of ours;
Work requiring so much labor,
 As to exceed our utmost powers.

" But He who said ' Go preach the gospel,'
 All powerful is, to aid, defend;
' Lo I am with you always,' said he,
 ' And will be even to the end.'

" With such command, and such a promise,
 Sure our path of duty's plain,
Do not then, dear friends, persuade us
 Longer with *thee* to remain."

Go then, go! we 'll not detain you,
We dare not ask your longer stay;
And may winds and waves of ocean,
Waft you safely on your way.

They who all forsake for Jesus,
Father, mother, country, home,
Here an hundred fold are promised,
And eternal life to come.

Go then, go! but when far distant,
Bear us sometimes on your mind;
When for others interceding,
Forget not those you leave behind.

And when your earthly warfare 's ended,
And you have laid your armor down,
May souls of poor benighted Asia
Add *many* stars to your bright crown.

TO MY HUSBAND.

Just two-and-forty years have passed *
Since we, a youthful pair,
Together at the altar stood,
And mutual vows pledged there.

Our lives have been a checkered scene,
Since that midsummer's eve;
Much good received our hearts to cheer,
And much those hearts to grieve.

Children confided to our care,
Hath God in kindness given,
Of whom five still on earth remain,
And two, we trust, in heaven

---

* July 11 1853

How many friends of early days.
Have fallen by our side,
Shook by some blast. like autumn leaves
They withered. drooped, and died.

But still permitted. hand in hand
Our journey we pursue,
And when we re weary, cheered by glimpse
Of "*better land* in view.

We may not hope in this low world,
Much longer to remain,
But oh! there s rapture in the thought,
That we may meet again

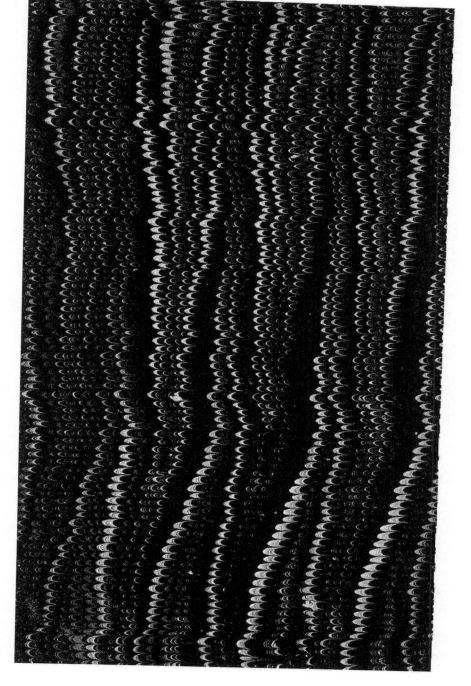

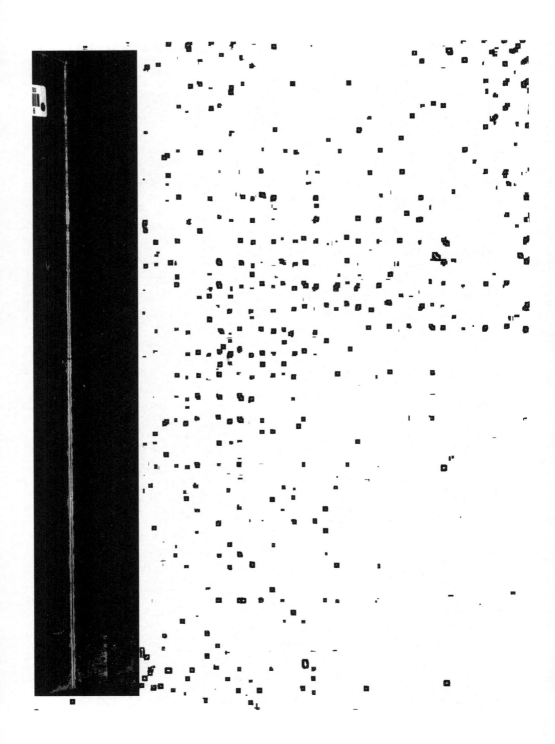

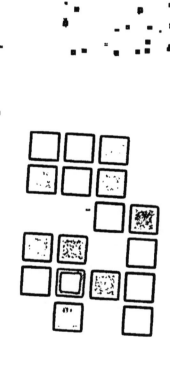

Lightning Source UK Ltd.
Milton Keynes UK
UKHW020644210721
387524UK00005B/232